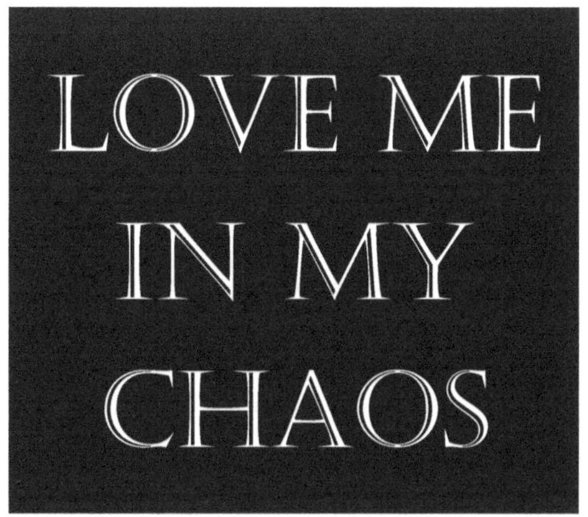

LOVE ME IN MY CHAOS

DINA AL HIDIQ ZEBIB

Poetry

LOVE ME IN MY CHAOS

First published in Belgium in 2018
by POLARIS INTERBUREAU
A Belgian Company

Photography
© 2018 Dina Al Hidiq Zebib
© 2018 Hussein Moussa Zebib
© 2018 Soraya Wazné
All rights reserved

Book Layout by: Dina Al Hidiq Zebib
Cover Design by: Dina Al Hidiq Zebib

Dina Al Hidiq Zebib
Email: dina@dinaalhidiq.com
Website: www.dinaalhidiq.com
Instagram: @dinahzebib

Paperback Edition
ISBN: 9782955861349

To my husband Hussein,
the love of my life and my soul-mate.
You knew how much I love to fly
so you helped me grow wings.
Ç'est toi qui me complète

To my boys, Faris and Amir,
my most precious treasures.
Your pride and admiration have kept me going.
You are my heart and inspiration.

FROM MY HEART TO YOURS

DINA HZ

"BE FOOLISHLY IN LOVE,
BECAUSE LOVE IS ALL THERE IS."

JALAL AD-DIN RUMI

"AND THOSE WHO WERE SEEN DANCING
WERE THOUGHT TO BE INSANE BY THOSE
WHO COULD NOT HEAR THE MUSIC."

FRIEDRICH NIETZSCHE

LOVE

2

You are…
a drop of water
to my dried lips,
a reviving pulse
to my sedentary muscle,
an endless shudder
to my ever-burning love.

"I watched you
while you were sleeping
and thought:
*How did I ever hurt
a beautiful angel,*"
he confessed
and apologized
while he kissed her hands,
her arms, her face, her lips…

"Come, let's climb this mountain.
I will show you a beautiful world,"
he told her as he reached out
to hold her hand tight.
"When we reach the top,
I will build you wings.
I want you to fly.
I want you to see the world
and soar above it all."
"But I'm afraid!" she cried.
"Don't be," he assured her,
"I will fly right behind you
and catch you if you fall."

❧ LOVE ❧

It was a night in *Getaria*
lonely and cold.
I sat by the sea port
watching the street lights
flickering on the boats
and the wild Atlantic waves
crashing onto the rocks.
I felt a presence.
I saw a shadow.
I heard his voice
whispering in my ear
tingling my skin
melting my heart
"I knew you'd come.
I believed you when you promised
that if our love kept burning
if the sparks kept glowing
you'd be here
one year after we'd met
and melted
in complete and utter passion
and burning love."

DINA AL HIDIQ ZEBIB

I lay down on the warm sand
under the hot *San Sebastián* sun
my head was in his lap
my hair through his fingers
my shoulders between his hands.
I closed my eyes
and smiled.
I was in one
of the many heavens
created just for me
and him.

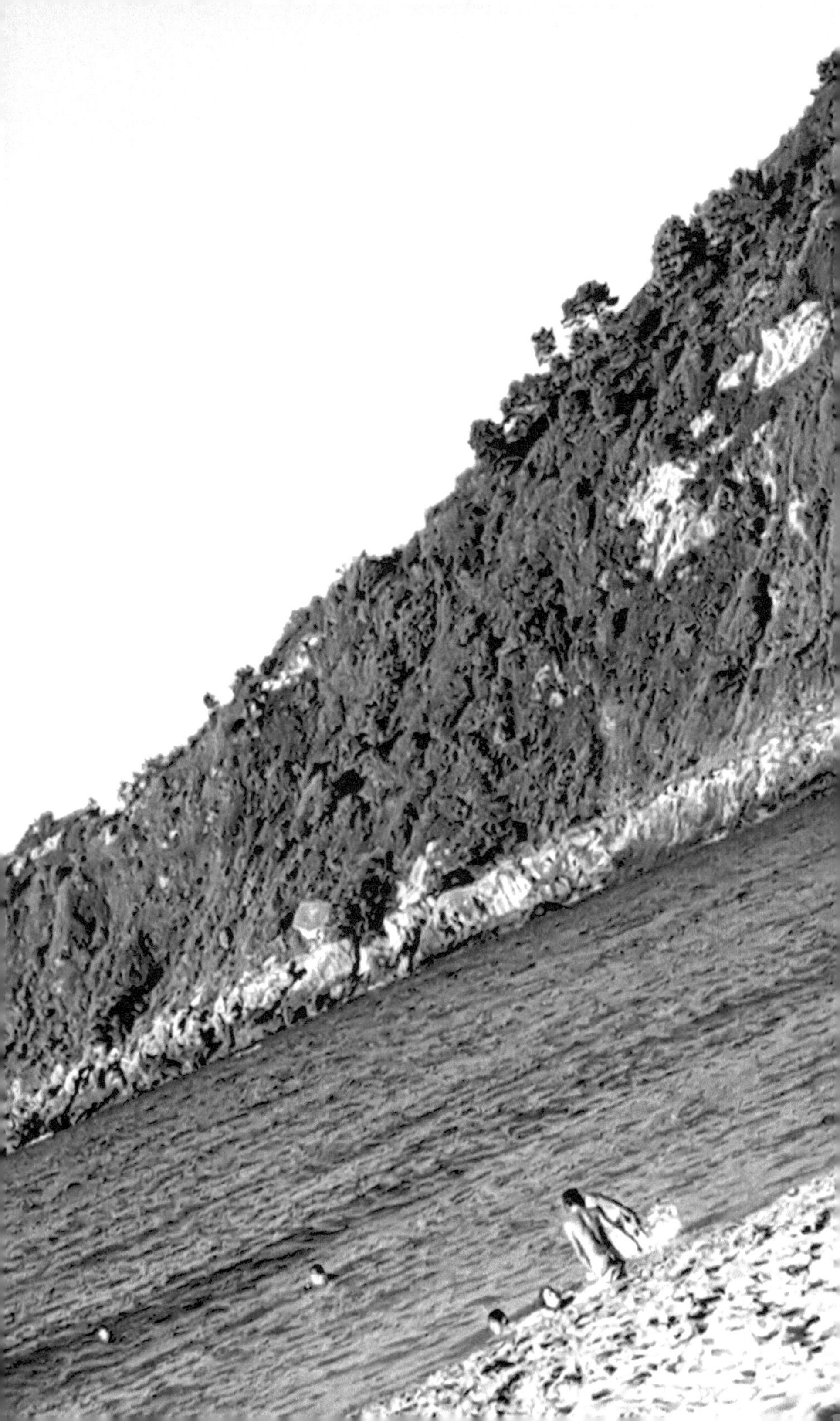

"Your love is my drug,
your taste is my wine
and you are my world.
There's absolutely nothing
I wouldn't do for you
to keep you safe and happy,"
he whispered in her ear
as he caressed her face
while she slept.

Whisper…
an emancipating wave
through my ear
grasping my veins
clutching my entire senses
I'm weakened
I quiver
ecstatic shudder
I'm besieged
I moan with delight
I'm the prisoner…
of your voice.

DINA AL HIDIQ ZEBIB

It's like a dream…
a wild, intoxicating dream
I don't want to wake up
yet I do
awaken to the reality of it,
physical awareness
not merely a mental captivation.
Sweep me,
uplift and alleviate me,
to a sky and star so high above,
for real now,
grasp my burning love
touch it, taste it,
delve into the growing burns
embrace my passion
squeeze me till it aches
the throbbing of truth
the truth that it's real
the dream turning to reality…

DINA AL HIDIQ ZEBIB

IF I TOUCH YOU,

I WILL RISK

BURNING.

I WANT TO BURN.

TURN ME

TO ASHES.

He poured me a glass of wine
while we sat by the fireplace.
He looked into my eyes
and spoke softly,
"I want to be your king
and your slave.
Will you be my queen
and my master?"

I want to walk
in the moonlight
and count the stars
off your face.

If you ever grow thorns,
sharp claws or fangs,
I won't fear you
and will keep on loving you
until the last breath
of my life,
because I know
you could never
ever
hurt me.

At this moment in time…
you're thinking of me
dwelling on every memory of our last encounter
breathing the scent of my existence
replaying every word we uttered to each other
reliving every fiery touch
gasping at the breathtaking sensations
gazing through your mind
at every lustful glance we gave each other
every ring of laughter we elicited
all a heavenly experience…
are you at this moment in time?

I saw him on the bridge standing above *La Meuse*.
He was on his phone,
his fingers running through his hair.
I gasped.
I knew him from a dream
from an ancient longing
an agonizing yearning
a mystic desire.
He must have heard my heart thumping hard and loud
because he turned around in my direction
like a magic compass
and he looked at me with his hypnotizing eyes.
His mouth ceased to move
his body stood still
his heartbeats drummed louder in sync with mine
and he spoke to me without uttering a word
"It's you I've been searching for my entire life."

The room was dark and crowded
the music deafening
she held his hand and pulled him close
as she swayed to the pulsing rhythm
and whispered,
"You wanted to be alone…
there's only me and you now,"
and they melted
into the darkness.

His eyes twinkled as he spoke,

"SHE IS

PERFECT

IN HER

IMPERFECTIONS."

If only I could find
the right words
to say
I LOVE YOU.

29

I feel so special,
safe and secure
in your presence
and so much more…
indescribable
unstoppable
oh so wonderful…
your mere existence.

DINA AL HIDIQ ZEBIB

So soft…
your presence, your air
I live off your scent
thriving on you.
Don't desert me
I'm aching at the thought
it's painful, torture
if you were to ever leave me.
I want your entire existence…
with me forever.

DINA AL HIDIQ ZEBIB

"Love hurts," said the little girl
tearful, broken
dwelling inside me.
"Yes, it does," I said.
"But only sometimes—not always.
Remember when that love was beautiful?
You will find love again.
Be patient. Be ready
because it's remarkably beautiful,
even if it might hurt."

DINA AL HIDIQ ZEBIB

I WILL LOVE YOU UNTIL

THE WORLD STOPS TURNING…

EVEN THEN,

MY SOUL WILL CONTINUE

TO BE WITH YOURS

How will it be…
when I'm alone again
left to a whiff of my past
that I thought was forever gone.
Please don't leave me
vulnerable, weak, sad.
Your existence yields mine
and you are my strength.
Exist here with me
I want you all
I want you even more…
you're my breath, my light…

…my life.

Hand in hand
we ran
in the *Ville Piétonne*
of *Louvain la Neuve*.
Like children
we laughed.
As lovers
we kissed.
In the dark alleys
we sneaked.
The chilly November night
echoed with our voices
our chuckles
our cuddles.
We were alive
happy
madly in love
and a little drunk.

DINA AL HIDIQ ZEBIB

Drowned in tears
he found me.
Close to his heart
he held me.
On a carriage ride
he took me
to show me
the shooting stars
the full moon
and the falling snow.
Snuggled in his arms
consoled by his love
soothed by the trotting
around the streets
of a magical Viennese night.

Love is feeling
never-ending breathlessness
it's wanting so much more
even when you have him all
it's breathing his scent in his absence
it's feeling his heartbeat forever strong
yet…

…love is so much more.

How you make me feel,
I shudder,
I shiver,
I'm overflowing
with love and desire
your soul is entwined with mine
and I'm quivering
what a marvelous flow.

DINA AL HIDIQ ZEBIB

42

My baby…
how I love you
breathless
exuberated…
lend me a breath
a whiff of air
tears suffocate me
negative consolation.
Stay

Baby
I love you so much
I can't bear fighting with you
hold me
forgive me
but you hurt me…

"She played
the keys of my heart,
gently yet sensually,
setting my soul on fire."

scen
do
sempre
cre
17

"SHE HAS BROKEN PIECES

THAT I WANT TO PICK UP.

SHE HAS SCARS

THAT I WANT TO MASSAGE.

SHE HAS TEARS

THAT I WANT TO KISS AND DRY.

SHE IS THE ONLY ONE FOR ME

AND I'M HERS

FOREVER."

I'm parched…
gasping…
ardent for a miniscule second
of admiring your eyes, mouth, skin
sensing your heat
holding you till I lose my breath
breathing your scent
tasting your lips
licking your skin
a fraction of a second
is all I need.

The beauties of life
can only be felt
with the heart

52

I'm having a vision
of you here beside me,
I'm engulfed in your arms
whimpering
moaning in delight.
I want you
here with me.

Glitter on my skin
twinkling in his eyes.
He reaches out
and traces a line
from my neck
to my shoulder…
glitter on his fingertips
fire in my soul.

DINA AL HIDIQ ZEBIB

54

I'm aching
so painful
so irritable
yearning
static, paralyzed by this
my reviving pulse
is you.
Baby, come back
once again be with me
never ever
leave me alone
ever again.

DINA AL HIDIQ ZEBIB

I'm waiting
burning with anticipation
to catch a glimpse of you,
to breathe your scent,
to touch your pulse,
to hold you…
I want to drown in your body
and lose consciousness…
never to be awakened
ever…

I'm yearning
to be alone with you
in our cabin by the sea.
I want to gaze at you,
to touch your face,
to breathe you,
to meld with your body,
with your heat
your voice,
oh, your voice
beautiful…so beautiful…so beautiful.

DINA AL HIDIQ ZEBIB

60

Darling,
you're my inspiration
a guardian angel
divine in your effect
Godlike is your existence
I'm overflowing
with your gushing river of emotions,
trembling
from the sensations
Continue…

His eyes pulled me in
his lips held me tight
his heart thumped hard
against my chest
and beat the clocks of time.

DINA AL HIDIQ ZEBIB

It was a
'Nice to see you'
kiss goodbye
that set my soul
on fire

❧ LOVE ❧

WITH EVERY VOICE I HEAR

EVERY FACE I SEE

EVERY HAND I TOUCH

I THINK OF YOU

AND CREATE MY OWN

LITTLE FAIRYTALE

DINA AL HIDIQ ZEBIB

I'm suffocating,
I wander like a ghost,
prickling with anticipation,
shuddering from your besiegement,
besiegement of my heart.
Sweet chill.

We walked into the room
the music was roaring
my head was buzzing
my heart pounding.
I held his hand
and pulled him in
so close
too close
symphonies playing in my soul
never wanting them to end.

DINA AL HIDIQ ZEBIB

His eyes on me
are committing a sin
that I don't want to stop

Assessing the graveness of my sin
as his eyes and lips pull me in
I graze his skin
with the side of my hand
shy at first
afraid for a moment
then…
submissive
as I await the blaze
that will burn me
inside out
until I scream
SWEET HELL.

His hands on my arms
his face next to mine
his breath kindling sparks
on my blazing senses.
He kissed my cheek
and lingered…
he took a whiff of my scent
and ignited
in my soul
a sensual fire.

DINA AL HIDIQ ZEBIB

I'm having thoughts of…
mothering you
with all my kindness,
protecting you
from all worldly perversions,
holding you
till the world sees no end,
cleansing your mind
from any disturbance,
praying day and night
for your contentedness and success
helping your every dream
turn to reality,
embracing your entire existence
with all my admiration,
dedication and affections.
I'm having these thoughts…
of you and me forever together,
such wonderful thoughts.

DINA AL HIDIQ ZEBIB

It was a night that time forgot
yet a vivid memory that haunts my heart.
I dream of you and it takes my breath away
I will love you forever…that is my legacy.

ME

Let me run wild and free
my heart needs to beat fast
my soul hungers to embrace the world
let me hold your hand
let's run together.

DINA AL HIDIQ ZEBIB

When you look at me and smile:
the earth stops spinning,
the clouds stop drifting,
the clocks stop ticking,
the wind stops blowing,
the pulse of the world stops beating
and I become
the queen of the world.

DINA AL HIDIQ ZEBIB

I walked into the room
and he looked at me.
The world came to a halt,
but the music started to play
the melody of my heart
strummed by his fingers.

Memories of you
have turned into daydreams
that control my every move
when I try to walk.
They dominate my mind
when I attempt to contemplate.
They govern my heart
when I struggle to breathe.
You are my destiny
and that…
I cannot escape.

LOVE ME
UNTIL THE FLAMES
OF THE LAST STAR
BURN OUT.

I used to dream
of the perfect life—
the life everybody wants—
until I realized
there is no such thing.
Perfection is personal,
it is how you see it,
how you want it to be.
My perfect life is how it is now
with you
with all the quarrels
and the tears…
with the moments of happiness,
the laughter
and the complete madness.

84

He said I would live
an adventure with him.
But I was afraid.
I wanted *safe*.
"Hold my hand.
I'll hold yours and never let go.
Trust me.
You will live the best life ever.
With me, you will always be safe."
And he was right.

86

I'm not drunk
nor high
I'm just happy
to be in love with you
so watch me dance
under the street light
and sing
to the twinkling stars.

THE OLDER I GET

THE BETTER I UNDERSTAND MYSELF,

THE MORE I EMBRACE MY FLAWS,

THE STRONGER I LOVE MYSELF,

THE BRAVER I BECOME,

THE HAPPIER I FEEL.

DINA AL HIDIQ ZEBIB

THERE IS NO BETTER WAY

TO FEEL HAPPIER

THAN TO BE CONTENT

WITH WHO YOU ARE.

IN AN AGE OF SPEED,

I PREFER TO STOP…

AND BREATHE IN

ANYTHING BEAUTIFUL

THAT I SEE.

92

"But where do you want to go?"
he asked her.
"I don't know.
Anywhere.
Just any place
where I can see
the sun rise
and feel the wind blow
and hear the sounds of the world.
My heart is restless
and my soul needs to wander
my senses want to roam the earth
everyday
until the day I die."

COULEURS
D'ÉTÉ

94

By the sea
is where I was born
where I grew up.
By the sea
is where my soul
comes back to life.

The greatest feeling
in the world
is to be able
to dance
to the music
that only I can hear.

With the avidity
of a starving nation
my soul yearns
to roam the world
to taste cultures
admire novelties
feast on beauties
and inhale
the love of the world.

You see my smile
you don't know that I hurt.
You read my words
you don't know that I struggle.
I don't hide behind rose-colored glasses.
I don't fake the smile that accompanies my tears.
I trip and fall
but I get up with hope.
I hurt and bleed
but I mend my wounds with love.
I let my tears roll down my cheeks
because it feels good to cry.
I get up again
a little stronger
a little wiser
and I try again
harder
because life is beautiful
and far too short.
I'll continue to see its beauty
I'll keep dreaming of the possibilities
and I'll never give up.
When life happens,
I'll keep on living.

Pour me a Prosecco
and watch me get drunk
give me your love
and watch me get high

The sun peaked at me
through the trees.
It winked
kissed my eyes
embraced my body
tickled my senses
soothed my burns.

I'm a romantic
roaming the world.
I don't know where to stop
or if I even want to stop.
I have a restless heart
and a thirsty soul
that only death will quench.
I never want to die…

The world tried to change me
and it did.
I became stronger;
I gained courage;
I developed confidence.
Life has taught me to embrace my flaws,
to love every minute of my life,
and to keep a smile on my face
because life is beautiful
and so am I.

DINA AL HIDIQ ZEBIB

It was a summer afternoon
in the city of Beirut.
I sat by the beach,
lazy, lonely, serene
toes buried in the warm, wet sand
legs massaged by the waves
skin kissed by the sun
hair caressed by the wind.
I gazed at the Mediterranean sea
and prayed…
for my heart
to remain as tender as the gentle wind,
for my mind
to be as intense as the scorching sun,
and for my soul
to grow dauntless as the gushing waves.

DINA AL HIDIQ ZEBIB

Seclusion
so wonderful
captivating spirits
queer to all
but to me,
I'm awestruck.

I am a strong, brave and free woman
who will stand strong against corruption
and demand justice.
I will fight against harassment, discrimination
and gender oppression
even when they try to savagely tear me down.
I will hurt, bleed and fall…
but only to nurse my wounds,
regain my strength
and sharpen my focus.
Then, I will get up,
head held high,
and I will fight again
with my words and wisdom,
my heart that can only love,
and my actions that speak of what is humane,
peaceful and just.
I am a strong, brave and free woman.
I am a Divine Warrior.

I sit idly waiting
for the waves of thought to fill my head.
They come in like a tide
bringing feelings, dreams, hopes.
The waves flow out of my pen
before my eyes
sensual verses
my mind laid out on paper.

DINA AL HIDIQ ZEBIB

I dreamed of everything beautiful
I listened to my heart
I chased my dreams
and spent most of my life
looking for my own fairytale
until I realized that
my life was already
the most wonderful fairytale
there could ever be.

It's so thrilling
to look into his eyes
and only see myself
dancing
to his heart beat
and swaying
to the melodies
of his soul.

Freedom is when your spirit
can flutter like a butterfly
with an abundance of happiness
in the open meadows of life
and rejoice in the little pleasures.
We are born to feel,
we aspire to be happy,
we thrive on love.
To be denied all this
is to be denied
our utmost freedom.

DINA AL HIDIQ ZEBIB

THE PULSE

OF THE ENTIRE WORLD.

IS ALL HERE

IN MY HEART.

❧ ME ❧

At the bar…
I close my eyes as I listen
my body curls with every breath
marvelous tunes captivate my mind
I am submissive to their power
I shudder and I tremble
I feel faint
but I want to move
my head starts to sway
my body bends along
I twist and curl like a slithering snake
my arms flow like the tidal wave
every melodious note is tickling me
pokes of pleasure
I rise above the ground
I float and flutter like a butterfly
I ascend to the sky, higher and higher
I drift in the air
happiness hovers over me
as I am detached from the world
it lasts for minutes but it feels eternal
the melody strikes its final note
I open my eyes as the feeling ends…

DINA AL HIDIQ ZEBIB

...I close my eyes and I listen again.

CHAOS

My emotions are constantly in turmoil
I overflow with feelings
that I don't always understand.
Come inside
get lost with me
embrace my chaos
thrive in my confusion
and I will wrap every inch of you
with my impetuous passion,
my breathtaking sensuality
and my never-ending love.

I'm full of knots
I'm a tangled mess.

124

"If you stay with me,
you will have to get ready
for a rollercoaster ride."
"Let's go."

I NEVER KNEW
WHAT I WAS DOING,
BUT I'VE ALWAYS KNOWN
IN WHICH DIRECTION
I WAS GOING.
BENSIMON
CONCEPT STORE

Don't be afraid to take risks.
Risk-free is boring—
it's like being buried alive.

Empty spaces
rooms of nothingness
shadows of the past
torture, pain…
they haunt me
disappearing slowly.
What remains is a growth
of spiritual longing
growing bigger and wider.
I see shadows of the future
a consoling hope
I await…to embrace.

Sometimes
I feel like
I'm the only
strange being
on earth.

Overwhelming fear
suffocation
lend me a breath,
a whiff of hope,
yet I want it real,
a hope of upcoming truth,
please be the truth
I want to breathe.

I'm so afraid
unexplainable fear, confusion
What? Endless interrogation…
Please, lend me an answer
help me through my chaos
I'm weakened by my ignorance
the ignorance of what I know
I know everything, but…I don't.
Confusion suffocates me
I want out
to finally stand and conceive
conception of my existence.
Rid me of my daze, of…
the quiver that dominates my soul.
Throw me the light
the light of darkness,
I need it…the light.

DINA AL HIDIQ ZEBIB

Constantly confused
scrambled words
entangled,
passionate,
my mind, my mind
I don't get how it is
why am I
so entangled…

❧ CHAOS ❧

DINA AL HIDIQ ZEBIB

WHERE IS MY VOICE

THAT SANG LULLABIES?

ALL I HEAR IS AN ECHO

OF A SOLEMN MASS.

DINA AL HIDIQ ZEBIB

❧ CHAOS ❧

By the *Dyle* I sat and wept
for my soul that has long been lost.
I searched the waters
and climbed trees.
I tilled the earth
and foraged leaves.
Bruised and broken
I heard a whisper
from the wind...the owl...the wild daffodil?
It spoke to my senses
and crept through my limbs
"I'm here where you left me—
parched...shrivelled...
but my pulse still beats.
Water me, revive me
with your tears and passion,
with your pain and laughter
I'll grow back stronger
and embrace you forever.

DINA AL HIDIQ ZEBIB

I used to feel like I was
dancing on the clouds.
Now, I just feel like
I'm smashed on the rocks.

Sometimes I feel
there is nothing more beautiful
in the world than
to get drunk
and laugh the night away.

Engraved
you are engraved in my skin
I am in yours
yet…
together we are not.

I'm walking,
I trip, I'm tripping,
uncontrollable
darkness…chaos…
Where? How?
Endless confusion
it's scratching, it's tormenting,
no strength, no light to revive me,
I'm drowning in a swamp of nothingness,
yet it is…something…everything…
wings…build me wings…
to fly…no,
to walk, just to walk.

DINA AL HIDIQ ZEBIB

My heart is tired
my love is limping
my mind is in chaos
my soul has run away
and I don't know
who can help me.

I stare at the River Seine.
Blankness.
All I feel is blankness.
Oblivious to the lovers passing by me
on the *Boulevard du Palais*
walking…hugging…kissing…
he left me here…
or I left him?
It must have been me and my madness.
But…
will we be reunited ever again?
Or is this the end?
I hear bells toll
from the *Notre Dame de Paris*
the sound strikes me like a blank note
an autumn breeze of what's to come
of the harshness of the winter chill.
Questions, confusion,
silent grinding pain.
Blankness.

DINA AL HIDIQ ZEBIB

I do not want to die
but sometimes
I wish I could sleep
forever

I close my eyes
and hear the sound of a choking violin
playing a sombre tune
that kills me softly.
I curl up in my bed
and tremble
from the agonizing memories.
The night is lonely
and black.
No consolation
not a star.
I'm broken
cracked open
dripping with pain
that drowns me
forever.

DINA AL HIDIQ ZEBIB

I travel to lose myself
in the beauties of the world
and to find my lost soul
within the chaos
of it all.

I sit in a café
in *Place Saint Lambert*
waiting for my heart to beat again
anticipating the sight of him
his scent
his voice.
Is he coming?
He promised he would
or was I delusional?
He wouldn't leave me,
or would he?
Men stop and smile
as I sip my vin de Liège.
They stare
awaiting an invitation
they're fools if they think
I could ever
give them a moment of my mind
a fragment of my heart
a cell from my body.
My mind, heart and body
are only for him
even if he decides
to leave me waiting forever
in a café
in *Place Saint Lambert*.

DINA AL HIDIQ ZEBIB

En Salle ou en Terrasse
Crêpes et Galettes
Maison
- Galettes Sarrasin :
Gruyère
Gruyère et Jambon
Complète
à la carte
- Crêpes Sucrées :
Sucre
à la Gelée de Violette
Nutella
Pomme au Beurre de Beurre et Sucre
Confiture
Flambée (Rhum ou Calvados)
Citron
Marron
No Carte crédit

The world never seemed so dry
The endless spaces of desert suffocate me
The burning sun mocks me
Its scorching rays blister my pale skin
I'm too frail to bare it
I'm too soft to deserve this
I squint into the distance
as I gaze at the remnants of a ruined civilization
one that had existed once in the very distant past
The structures still stand tall
but they are withered from the atrocities
Those who breathe cruelty and greed
Their hearts have been scorched by the raging sun
They are as black as darkness and as hard as steel
We are strange to them, pure, chaste, and despised
We do not belong here, nor should we ever try
We never want to try.

DINA AL HIDIQ ZEBIB

We are of another kind much different from theirs
one that feels love, concern, and fear
We fear the darkness of evil souls
We feel remorse at the slightest hurt
We thrive on love and being loved
We love mankind, each other, and ourselves
We love our Almighty God and we fear His fury
I cannot survive here
I grasp onto my final breaths
as I await relief, to be released again
to be liberated into the world I once knew
a beautiful world I once loved.

DINA AL HIDIQ ZEBIB

I wish I could disappear
and not have anyone miss my presence
but it cannot be
I wish my existence would stop
and my trace in life gone
but it should not be
I wish I could pause my pain forever
until the end of lifetime
but it would not be
I wish I could stop feeling, thinking,
and breathing the confusion
but it shall not be
I wish my suffering could stop
and pleasurable feelings return
but it does not seem to be
I wish life could be simpler
and problems more solvable
but how can that be…

DINA AL HIDIQ ZEBIB

...I wish I could blend in the winds
of a peaceful realm
but it cannot ever be
I wish I could bury myself in white soil
and sprout as a daffodil
but it would never be
I wish my dreams for a better life for all mankind
could come true
but it will not be
I wish hatred and envy
could be demolished across the entire earth
but how will it be
I wish my life was different
and people were better
but that will never be
I do not wish to endure my suffering
nor witness human immorality...

...but that will eternally be.

WHAT DO I SEE?

DARKNESS CONQUERS

DRYNESS LINGERS

REMARKABLE

I feel dry
not a single drop of soul left

As I look through the window
the wind blows my hair
I feel my heart is grabbed and stabbed
the pain rivets my heart beat to a jolt
I feel a dash of agony race through my body
it pores through my veins
it aches me all over
my stomach churns, it twists and turns
my body throbs
I cannot bear the anguish
my mind cries for mercy.
Dear God help me.
Eradicate my misery.

DINA AL HIDIQ ZEBIB

"Speak.
What's wrong?
Why are you different?
Why have you changed?"
How could I speak
when the lump in my throat
is choking me
blocking my voice
crushing my heart
and killing me slowly.
I speak with my eyes
that drip tears of blood
sucked out from my heart.

"But I don't understand you,"
he cried.
"You never will
and you don't have to,"
she explained. "Just love me
the way I am,
because even though
you don't understand me,
all that matters is
for you to understand
that my love for you is
as deep as the ocean
as wide as the galaxies
as solid as the mountains
and as fierce as the wind.
That is all you need to understand.
Just love me…

…love me in my chaos."

DINA AL HIDIQ ZEBIB

"I LOVE HER,
AND THAT'S THE
BEGINNING AND END
OF EVERYTHING."

F. SCOTT FITZGERALD

ABOUT THE
Poet

DINA AL HIDIQ ZEBIB
is an award-winning Author, Poet
and Positive Psychology Coach.

She was born and raised on the Eastern Mediterranean coast. She spent her childhood travelling the world with her parents and siblings, which instilled in her a love for different cultures, a fascination with the world, a need to explore, and a positive outlook on life. All these experiences allowed her to develop a deep sense of sensibility and sensuousness that she expresses in her writings. She lives in Belgium with her husband and two children. She spends every opportunity she has to write and to travel with them.

For more information, visit:
www.dinaalhidiq.com
Instagram @dinahzebib

ABOUT THE
Images

Photos in this book were captured by the author and her husband during their travels, with the exception of five photos (pages 13, 35, 77, 145, 153) which were taken by Soraya Wazné—a very talented teenage girl who is very precious to the author's heart.

The locations where the photos were taken are:

Santorini, Greece; Pissouri, Cyprus; Beirut, Lebanon; Vienna, Austria; Brussels-Atomium Square, Mont-Saint-Guibert, Walhain, Louvain-la-Neuve, Wavre, Ottignies, Court-Saint-Etienne, Dinant, Liège, Bruges, Knokke-Heist, Recht, Belgium; Monaco; Paris, Deauville, Bordeaux, Nice, Èze, Saint-Paul-de-Vence, Tourettes-sur-Loup, Cannes, Villefranche-sur-Mer, France; San Sebastián, Getaria, Zarautz, Sanctuary of Loiola, Basque Country, Spain.

The author was inspired to write her poems either while visiting or staying in those locations, or from inspirational moments that touched her deeply during those travels.

The models in the images wish to remain anonymous.

From the
hearts & souls
touched by

LOVE ME IN MY CHAOS

Poetry

Love Me In My Chaos
is a stunning collection of poetry and photography
that explores the themes of love, longing, sensuality,
femininity, passion, happiness, and togetherness.
Beautifully written, with heartfelt and profound
emotions, Mrs. Zebib's touching poems will resonate
with anyone who is a romantic at heart and dreams of
getting lost in the harmony of love.

—Alexandra Vasiliu, Poet. USA

Dina's Poetry
takes us on a journey deep into her soul. Her poems
touch us and remind us that we all want to understand
others, but more importantly also want to be
understood.

—Dr. Ramola Vengsarkar, Artist. India-Belgium

Love Me In My Chaos
is very personal, sensual yet romantic, purely
simplifying the essence of love. A reminder much needed
in our times of chaos.

—Gala Borisova, Singer & Poet. Bulgaria

❦

Love Me In My Chaos
is a beautiful collection of inspirational poems based
on love and life that is written elegantly and from the
heart. Each poem takes you on an amazing journey of
love, hope, faith and strength.
The book shows that even when life gets you down, even
when we lose hope in difficult situations we can still get
back on our feet and transform into someone even
stronger. The beautiful imagery in her book allowed me
to probe deeper into her descriptive writing which made
each poem seem even more real. I felt lost in her poems
and could easily relate on different levels. A very
engaging and captivating book that made me want to
read more and more.

—*Lena Salha, Author of Semi-colon(;). Australia*

❦

www.ingramcontent.com/pod-product-compliance
Lightning Source LLC
La Vergne TN
LVHW042106190726